Love and Other Distractions

Maurice Spillane

 **WRITERSWORLD**

United Kingdom : France : Germany : Spain

Love and Other Distractions
Maurice Spillane

All rights reserved

Copyright © 2004 Maurice Spillane

Maurice Spillane is hereby identified as author of this work in accordance with Section 77 of the Copyright, Design and Patents Act 1988. No part of this publication may be reproduced, stored in a retrieval system or transmitted in any form or by any means, electronic, mechanical, audio, visual or otherwise, without prior written permission of the copyright owner. Nor can it be circulated in any form of binding or cover other than that in which it is published and without similar conditions including this condition being imposed on the subsequent purchaser.

ISBN 190418158-9

Cover design by
www.tinracer.com

Photo by Judith Kruger

Layout and typesetting by
www.dwrobinson.com

WRITERSWORLD
9 Manor Close
Enstone
Oxfordshire
OX7 4LU
England

www.writersworld.co.uk

Printed and bound by CPI Antony Rowe, Eastbourne

Also by Maurice Spillane:

Saying Poems
All Aboard Who Are Coming Aboard
Love in a Time Warp

The poem *Pedro*, first appeared in *The Naked Leader*
by David Taylor, published by Transworld.

For Fiona

Table of Contents

Love

And then, a blossoming,
A stretched awakening

Bad Times

You say: move on now without fuss,
in that all passing passes thus,
hug to forget, just don't say us -
all change, all change, there is no us.

Reflection

I have found the godhead and it is myself —
I am the dancer, the dancing and the dance.

Dead and Dying

He's in a sleep warp.
For us, still the damp white knuckles and
Snow curls. Quiet now.

Travels

But I can see him still,
That forward face, the slip-streamed hair,
Two hands wrapped braces, a charioteer.

Children

And Dad, even though you're gone,
is she still my sister?

And . . .

Some day a Goddess will unlatch this gate

Love

And then, a blossoming,
A stretched awakening --

Love and Other Distractions

When

I hate the indecisiveness of it,
When to put your arm around her shoulder,
Hold her hand, touch her hair,
Fold her gently, so very gently
Like fine china, that kind of gentle.
She looked so good tonight.
The stitch in her sweater –
I watched it unravel, urged to pull,
To hurry the unravelling
As if travelling that endless path
Might lead to a consequence,
Might lead to knowing when.

Anyway

I don't know if it matters much
That equidistant is a confluent set,
Or that influence has no distance,
Or that intimacy mocks both.

Anyway.
It does matter that someone cares
Enough to stare enough beyond,
To undress with the eye, stroke with the nose,
Reach even-handed into the mind.

Anyway, that's what I thought then,
Think now to be honest,
So close and so intimate,
As far as a stick in a river,
A stick that can't be reached,
So near only half described,
And a lifetime other half.

Anyway, who cares if there are
Many sliding paths to the soft place -
This confluence of intimacy
That holds no bars, that bars no holds,
That leans into a wind from both sides.

Who cares? Well, I did and that's true.
Maybe cared too early,
Like picking apples in spring,
The absurd becoming reality
As the year raced to an end.
Anyway, that's what I thought then.

And then, a blossoming,
A stretched awakening –
Not a big spark or an earthquake,
Not ambient intrigues,
Not any of the 'nots' really,
Just perfect alignment,
Our sleepy caucus that
Defines contentment,
When reaching out is reaching in.

Anyway.
That's how it feels now.

She is Left-Handed

She is left-handed –
Think about that.
Think about cutting bread with a very sharp knife,
Or turning a page, or counting notes,
Or tying a lace, or dishing out mash,
Or brushing her teeth, or massaging your throat,
From the left-hand side.

She is left-handed –
Each statement a tripwire
Of half-breath deliberations,
Of unfinished sentences,
And then the distant gaze
And the deviation down some ferreting hole,
Holding everyone's attention,
But not through conversation,
Oh no, it's a heartfelt wish that she'll come back.
And everyone's too polite to ask
If left-handed people are all like that.

She is left-handed –
When we met she slept on the left,
Announced some ownership rights,
Some distorted set of back to front,
But a moment of surrender
Sent her over the edge,
And now she sleeps on the right side of the bed,
Where women usually sleep -
Especially when they are with men.

She is left-handed –
Which requires tolerance from me
When she rattles my ordered world.
Now I buy fish and chips for two,
And the wine is gone about half way through,
But it's touching glasses left to left
That really messes up my head.
And she says she loves me,
Like she means it,
Like it might be true,
Like a left-handed person might say it,
Who hasn't quite worked out
How wonderful it is to be
With someone disturbingly wonderful.
That's she.

The Circle at Bath

The guide led us into the circle of trees,
and said: *Hear how the noise abates,*
and said: *Two trees are long now dead,*
but strange,
I have never known it so quiet here before.

The circle is now complete.
I brought two giants across the street,
one is tall and beautiful,
the other, I homage at her feet.

Bridges to Home

But love's not lost if time ignored,
Perhaps new voices from the west,
Softer voices, carrying spores.
Perhaps ignoring spawns a nest.

So much lost, so much retained
A cornucopia for the brave,
Little grandeurs explained
By chucking stones into a grave.

I turn my face full to the wind,
Then turn to face the land,
Then turn again to start my trip,
The steps to where I stand.

A Summer Tryst

We are Gargoyles on hanging buttes of sand,
A chasm climb. Our decade friendship strains
The convention of accepted claims,
Like first cousins, or the unwashed, or contraband,

Or knotted vesper brows that whisper *shan't*.

Gargoyles do not desire a summer tryst,
But we do. You from your perch, I from mine,
Untouched, unheard disciples of Descartes,
I palm your tossled hair, your lips unkissed.
A slip of knots - the landing could be fine –
But we are, of now, a foot or two apart.

What Happens When it Doesn't Happen?

Sauces beat me. Some are easy to make
from a packet. But beaten eggs sweating
over steam are much more attractive
with their slightly lumped, not
quite better taste.

I once made love for hours with no result.
The no result was not important then,
a minor act in a long play of acts
that moved the trappings
that were hiding my boundary.
Beyond that even. It was like being
at school with a great teacher
and not wanting the bell to ring,
tossing out a word to prolong.

I think of that as my quiet anointing, the
perfect resonance of touch and saying things,
so simple when you are shown how.

For example,
I have tried a hundred times to fold
caramel over a spoon and nest some fruit.
Sometimes the caramel is too hot,
sometimes the spoon is not chilled enough,
sometimes every time it nearly works.

Except once, in a cafe kitchen
a pastry chef spun a spoon
and showed me how to make it work.
Once. Just like that other once.

Reflection

I'm looking at the lake above a lake
Above a pond, the plant-pucked waterfall,
And the visitors splattering playful,
Wary as we would never need to be
Like sentries stop-start chewing on the sly.

I wonder if I, on another day,
Could have foreseen this creation take shape:
the water-slush hugging my aching spade,
mud-slick mounds from a pattern in the ground,
the sculpt-patted edge – a natural edge.

It has turned out all right. You said so.
The depth holds the water, the banks are firm,
And when seepage comes from birds flying in,
Some finger pressing and it's right again.

If there's an after-life, as there is now,
I wonder if we'll be allowed, you and I,
to set the scenes the way we have been,
lakes within lakes, the way we enjoy.

A Birthday Card

In the unexpected quiet of your office day
Take down this milestone birthday card,
And hold the thought that this was once
A continuous flow of castellated ink –
Despite the pitch, like a storm dragged ship
Trying hard to find the leeside of words that
Would best celebrate the passion in which I hold you,
Know that there will be a moment
When one birthday will be half a milestone.

How the years will have flown –
How they fly now as we read of dates in your book,
And of words that seem to have chiselled good time
In the face of all that we strove through. Toss me
My new suit and braces and my devilish air;
Pass me the keys of the Jag and the fine cigar
That I will smoke over a quiet beer and a great book!
And take me around our house again and in a mute
Moment reflect the magic of a genteel day,
As we skirt the paths that took all summer long.
We have gilt more lilies that we ever knew.

And what of these for you, who are never still?
The best reflecting the best, like focus group mirrors
That make the drama last, with you outside the room;
Or perhaps you will break custom this time and enter
To confront the disarming you that only our bedroom knew.

It cannot be the ironing mountain, or the daily chores,
Or cooking evening meals, or reflecting on a political day.
Perhaps it is the nesting that you build for me and little you.
There is more to make you trip so easily with so much glee.
It cannot be things so simple, so why does it mystify me.

There will be a time to dust this card and, reading it,
Think fondly that once there was a heartbeat where I lay
My head on your breast, ruminating these runes
Of our time, as a manifesto for us of whom we are now.
Pause then to catch your sense of us as we wander
In the unexpected quiet of your office day.

Time over Habit

We are building our nest nicely.
Each pile, each lintel is cut to plan
and bolted through, lichen-ready,

solid as the meandering
paths without the house that lead you
maze-foot, and guide you back again,

solid as the break of colour
where rooms and stairwells interleave
and glide willing eyes from pigment
to construction, like a Renoir,
always easy, always a surprise.

The years have added depth to our
chorus, loose sure,
uncontriving, aery voices,
settling into their own demise.
We even get our dates mixed up
interlacing habit into time.

A few score years from now
I wonder if we'll say about these days:
was that the year we married,
or was it the year before?

Cutting Back the Trees

I climbed up the tree and when I was high
decided I should have taken a rope
or a thick belt for support. Dead and live
I cut with macho nonchalance using
a handsaw made for more delicate work.
The big boughs thudded down, bucked and crashed
the fence and lay on the bare earth. Snappy
little branches fussed back like troubled thatch.
Sweaty smells, and cuts and I'm puffed up happy.

I can see how this garden will be. Drills
for the big roots and beds for peas, frilled
herbs and edging so they look good from
the window. Fenced off mulch. A garden
plot needs compost as the best living
seems to come from recycling the dead things.

There's a sense of being there to get here.
The wild African garden where I reared
the gardener with the garden. The ruin
that was Wicklow where scutch grass ran amok
and life was a young colt and then got stuck.
Dublin, boxed, like a window box boxed in.

This will be a different plot. Wander
paths will surprise with turns to safe retreats,
each a frescoed chancel without a priest,
where we can be alone among the crowd
and they can take as much as they do now.
Why not?
　　　　　We'll have more than we'll ever need.

Comfort

Take the rucsac for example.

You searched the pockets
For something safe
But did not test the torque
Of how big that space could be.
Very silly.

If you are surprised
Reach across the bed
And put the light out.
Or add to the books on your side
Page by page
For I am already asleep.

You can see me as I am,
Safe in my snore,
Awake in my asleep,
Letting butterflies out
Through my lips –
Hap clappy wings
That radiate the dark
And drift carefree
Around the warmth of our being.

You think you cause
The sun to rise?
Ask my butterflies
Who are already at the window
When you wake,
Exorcising the night,
Welcoming the day,
Blowing words on to the wallpaper
To make more space for us
Until we encase ourselves in sleep again,
In this our special room again,
Strangers beyond ourselves.

After a Discussion on Politics

There are not answers enough
nor questions enough to fill our time.

And there you are, lovely
in these formative years for you –
seeking as if each decade was
your first year. I cannot form
such exuberance easily now
but I remember how it was,
bursting for a thought,
outflanked by words,
hands gesturing in the gap,
beseeching an understanding
so the next point can be played.

I wait like a cat, giving you hope,
allowing you to travel full circle
and then telling you so with gusto.

I enjoy the kill too much, even if
I am regurgitating from a read piece,
solid as the footnotes and their fractions.
But to win is all it is. A middle ground
would allow you no respect.

I am watching you now,
like big brother, weaving what you say,
forming pictures from around the edge
and feeling for the gem of the unsaid,
knowing, like Merlin, that when unleashed
the shield wall will be broken and the
Celt and all his villainy will be slain.

Your Birthday

And here is that annual time to agonise again.
What to get for you. I will get a present somewhere
but that is just a physical thing,
more a pampering for the moment,
with a shelf life only slightly longer than its wrapping.
What can I give you that is beyond the milestone,
without the constraining symmetry of one?

If I had it in my power I would give you your dreams.
If I had them at my command I would bring you hordes
to adore you, to royal respect you as you are.
If I had gods to plunder, their treasure would be empty.
If there were horizons to curtail you, I would lay them flat.
If your ambitions were fulfilled, there would be endless clapping.
If I had magic, these words would flow to honour you.

I do not have that power. Last year
I did not need glasses. How quiet it is.

The best I can give you is attention, an audience of one,
an adoring audience for that, charmed by your tales,
ennobled by your charm, reflecting at best the best in you.
I can be a wedge to enable your ambitions, to crave
as you should crave for what is your rightful due,
to distract the threats of obvious intent and panga a path
through the gratuitous distortions of seeing what can be seen.
I could at best be your St. John, pampering your way
with word petals, interpreting the riddles of what will be.
This at least I can wrap and watch the wrap unfurl,
and hope that what falls out is more than bumbling words.

Then

If I could remember when we really met,
I would know why the little things that changed
our lives so easily passed me by. Then.

Did we treasure in hours or days
the moment when we knew we worked,
or did we back-flush our history
from the moment that we touched.

Maybe we incarnate the time when
time itself was still, captured in a capsuled
frame with sepia ageing and wonder-filled.

Perhaps there is no beginning, as there is no end
to what we have and what we built. The past
is just a bridge from here to there, built in
seamless beams from now to then.

Jottings within an Office

I should stand again on Dublin hills,
blustered by the wind. That day.
I was a hill upon a hill;
beneath my fingers I could feel your tap, tap,
watch the waves bash at the bay,
see the heather crease against the bog
and your hair blasted around your face,
and above in the blue sky, higher than I, nothing.
I am the pinnacle, your hand in my hand,
a Celtic Moses waiting for the word.

It is a mischief to challenge the shadows.
How easy to face the gods on a clear day,
we who are here, we who belong.

We step down by the rusty wire
and walk the ruts they call a path
and stop where the pony backs into the wind,
you and she and me; life on life on life.

I fill still with the winds that blew that day
as hand on hand on hand we circled our corral;
these, the same winds, that merge our thoughts
so we think as we feel and sometimes say
to confirm the miracle that is us;
these, the same winds, that step us from our hills
and let me lie quiet beneath the sovereign you
and take from your mighty calm into my fire.

Home Again

We are no accident, you and I. Ships may pass
but today, when I returned from a business trip,
it was the coming home, the comfortable locking
of a shunting, the perfection of a universal joint.

When I left I was already deducting the time,
wishing the time away, breathless that the grass
would grow (your meadow seed), the daffodils
would be off-bloom, the paths disintegrate, aged
like the beard that needs a shave after a shave –
moving right along – I will it for my foreign self
but want your temple there to freeze in time.

And then the deliciousness of a messed up drink,
laughing at the silliness in us, who slopped
the slop and who should mop. Your hair cut short
to open your youth again. How far indeed
from structured business frames and the cold
format of a spreadsheet. As far as freedom
from indenture. These your lips. Home again.
And these the tips of my fingers, sticky stained
from dancing over you when I missed you most.

Spring Haiku

Tying daffodils
below the heads of dead yellow -
this Spring for next Spring.

April Fool

This is my hotel room – midnight –
and this is where I now am at.
Today I played executive
and hungered for you. Tonight I
look at your note and think I know you.

What are we doing? Trying
to make love through the
glass wall of our distance with hands
that cannot touch, lips that cannot kiss.
Two dreams of escaping so easily escape –
escape into a dream. Do you dream?
Do you dream by day
of how we may or may not be?
It is dangerous to dream by day, for
I want to be your mind, your body,
my hands in places where only poets go.

We have no reference to compare except,
except the moments that we polish for ourselves.
Dream dreams of Africa and Tibet,
jumping from stalled ships if we are let;
jump, if we can jump, when we jump, when...

Let me see deep from inside your gaze.
Somehow these will soon be quaint old days,
For tomorrow is where we are at.

I Glimpse Your Mind

I glimpse your mind between our wane and waxed
Romance. After the meal I saw your face
Clouded with thoughts unsaid – unsaid has taxed
Us in our newness. Saved by an embrace,

We tipped around the argument with grace,
For we are too new at this, and before
We walked the rapids into a deep place
Hands protect where requited words might score.

We loved emprise on bed, in shower, on floor
Two aerobic kids, curkling when we must.
This is our solution: attend the sores
Before they burst with touch and taste and thrust.
If we can tame words to honour us best,
Imagine the decades we could harvest.

You Gave Me Colour and Dance

All day I fingered a canvas to
Paint you in rhyme. Around are songless birds.
When the sun is down everything is grey.
You gave me colour and dance;
                                        I only words.

Black is the mood of the poet apart.
How can I paint a receding day,
And shadow our footsteps between the
Shingle and shore.
                        Quietly the waves fade.

Then you phoned. What brightness in *hello*.
The pen and paper glow in your dark hue.
I have no reality in shadows.
The canvas itself is reflecting:
                                I love you.

I will paint you in a dance. Hands held high
And fingers tangoing your vertebrae.
I am a sunflower following your sun.
And when we meet tonight,
                        Colour my day.

Making Love in the Afternoon

You are embarrassed, you say,
Standing in a strange flat, in someone else's sunlight,
Questioning a night-time activity by day.

You pull down the curtain to keep the voices out.
We whisper and fondle words to find our old accord
And ease our clothes and settle down to touch.

We close out the nether world and open up each other.
You give permission and I grow in you
Enveloping you like a Russian doll.

Our bodies rock to a single pulse
Stirred by the vein inside your rooted grip,
Hungering wild, and deep, to lose control and

Scream your love-cry. Help me scream mine
Like a lion roaring terror across an African plain.
This is ours alone. This is our primeval game.

Love eases gently back to hushed words, to slush
And touch and taste and make-believe.
Lying in this strange bed. We are not pretending now.

Baby-sitting with Elgar and Candles

And on this night I sat down to write.

Elgar brooded around me and I lit
five candles to torture the mood.
In the kitchen, supper is ready and I even
made some dressing and supped and played
and supped again to get it right.

I feel you whispering in this room:
Write me a poem. Just like that.

I unwrapped more cheese than two can eat.
This is a treat: sitting at home waiting for you.

It took ages to dry the lettuce in the tea towel,
but now I think it is too dry.
I will put down this pen
and wet the lettuce again.
It has to be just right.

This Thought

Hold this thought.
Cup it in your hands like a precious jewel.
Lift it slowly to the sun like a priest at the consecration.

These are your exalted palms
and this is your life breath,
blowing slow-motion
and scattering the thought like dandelion seeds
that glimmer and sparkle the sun stream
and hang without gravity.

I will pluck every seed
and fold them back into your hands,
exchanging in smiling benediction
the order of giver and receiver.

In our temple, the angry shades
are pushed back; only fingerprints
remain on the soft wood
where they tested the grain and found
we had woven around our strains of
softness with lovers' knots.

For there is in this thought a joining
that powers shut like a clam:
this is the hard shell around the softness
of you in your tripping unsure
and me, not allowing interruption,
admonishing with conviction from my mudslide.

And the thought of consistency,
this thought of being us as we are,
holds well and binds us well.
We are disparate objects using
speech to caricature what we were,
when what we are, we are:
you with your good sense fondling our embrace,
the priestess that offers up with graceful humour,
and I simply seeing you each day for the first day.

I Just Got Back

There is a sorrow in the timbre of voices
where the gaps are furrows in a ploughed field,
you atop the drill, defining your space with your tossed clothes
and I in the hollow agonising over loss and gain.

I feel your isolation in this room while I was away.
There is a grief that crawls around my back
as if it had shadowed your pain, your aloneness.
My back is against the radiator and still shudders the cold.

You phoned to say welcome home, rushing between
your other guests leaving and the cars leaving;
a hurried 'hello' and Laraesque in its joy.
There is a sneakiness still in reaching out.

How I love that voice. What is the sound that words
cannot emulate? Is it the ancient call?
Reach out to me like that, embrace me through
the telephone wires. These are the sounds of joy.

Tomorrow you will glad my day. Eleven, you say.
Tomorrow we will rush our arms and hands and
scream in our rehearsed play and fence words around
the significance of you and me. We will okay again.

In tonight though, I watch TV and waste away the hours
plucking channels as a sop to being entertained.
This house might be warm with you but I cold it
by gnawing the hope that alone is not alone forever.

I just got back from Ireland and already, but slowly,
I am opening out of my protected self. There is a freshness.
There is the whole that the timbre of your voice released,
and, in releasing, allows me to be me. I just got back.

Being You

The simple things:
candles of all sizes perfectly misplaced,
even the tulips droop to your order.

Like attention,
when magic tingles in your fingertips
and you give the memory of a memory
of sunset and song and unfettered dreams.

Like the way you smile
with your eyes. There is no guard there.
Your being is a cherub willing the immediate
to share the innocent in your eyes.

You are as you are
with the world your amused audience,
glad to adore in the chorus,
glad to share a heartbeat and travel your note.

A Big Day

You are away now,
like a child on her first day at school:
a little pensive, trying out your new shoes,
wondering if the tent will collapse on you.

It will not, at least not today.
You are wise and hearty now and
full of wonder as I once found you.

Enjoy your day.
Savour it well; a new day to treasure
like no other day. You will not recall
the next few jumbled rolling days.

But today is a special day,
another day for the rest of your life.

You Make My Day

You make an occasion out of nothing.
What charm is that? The electronic mail
is full of instances that fill your day,
seeing people for what they are, or are not,
wise and observant, silly and unsure in their mirrors:
not them, perhaps, but you.

You are on the phone rambling as if to a script
and I blunt the calm with exact sentences.
I hate the instrument and it knows it, distorting
my feelings by sending my voice in a straight line.
You just glide along the waves as if you two were one:
not it, perhaps, but you.

On Saturday I will be home. Forget the phone.
Are you agonising now, parading now, over what to wear?
I know a recipe will have been recycled for days and days.
You will conceive it from nowhere.
Plucked between candles.
And words, at last, will blend with loving,
and touch will endure:
not mine, perhaps, but yours.

Winter Song

The essence of strife is life itself,
scattered dreams without a sunrise.

Write a poem, you said,
to sublimate the mind in you.

Let me play with oil, you said;
let me bring life from your life,
let me smile a child from the man again.

It is my birthday soon, you said,
so let us revisit the simple things:
a business trip to Venice again,
one year on from then again.
Is the parchment seller any older?
Is St. Mark's Square still there?
Are the dream desires we rhymed
in children's riddles giggling still?
Will the Winter sun still peak at noon?

For my birthday, internal rhyme us,
you and I, into our poem, you said,
so I sat to sculptor words on you and me.

And you and I are in our own sun
that everything else just rattles around.
The sun will rise even if I am asleep again.

The Christmas Tree

The wind is blowing high this Christmas Eve.
In the dank greyness of an English night,
The pines and yew and spruce suck in the light,
And the dark swirls around like a whelk sleeve.

Candles hug candles inside reflections,
dancing the shadows. There's music and beer:
Guinness for Santa and carrots for deer
a wangle of warmth and expectations.

You created this when the tree was done –
Then stooped to see it from a small child's view.
Disassembled it and started anew
By re-assembling to her horizon.

It was painful putting it together,
Lights that never work and then somehow do,
Baubles unwrapped then blended into hues
Of cribbed and crafted chippings of pleasure.

And then you took the Christmas tree apart
To start again, and if in truth I tell
That I completely missed what you could feel
And missed even more that *it's from the heart*

As if some great event had come that night
And I was there and saw every movement
But seeing, saw nothing in the rapid rent
Of a tree from good to bare to *now it's right.*

I wish that I had taken photographs
Of each unpeeling, each considered build,
Each bauble's careful placement as you filled
Each empty space with your peculiar craft.

She will remember it though, panoply
Of time through time through circumstance
To her own child's Eve. Her inheritance
Is that you viewed the view and not the tree.

Dreams

And what are dreams?

Bits and pieces of flotsam
washing up on the beach,
dancing in time to the
virtual motion of waves;
forever in touch,
forever in line.

Catch my fingertips and
dance with me.

Love and Other Distractions

Bad Times

You say: *move on now without fuss,*
in that all passing passes thus,
hug to forget, just don't say us -
all change, all change, there is no us.

Bringing the Forest Home

How come we never noticed the dead leaves
Before we got the driveway paved.
The newness ruined it, made the dirt stand out,
Made it stand out like lumps of clod
That traipse up the stairs when you come in
From a run, and carefully clean on your way down;
Made it stand out like hard words that sour
And you wish they could be taken back
But there is no Kleenex for taking-back.

I thought of how the forest follows me around.
I went for the paper: three long steps
From the front door to the mail-box and back,
And when I closed the door six leaves were there,
Not in any order, just placed on the carpet,
Placed in places that I hadn't trodden,
Placed by whom, and how? There was no wind,
And I was careful where I stepped,
And I didn't rush the door to swirl them in.

Special leaves. I picked them up and
placed them on a sheet and saw veins and bruises
and bits of leaf bit out. There must have been a fight,
or maybe the long drop from the tree,
Or maybe it was I, brushing and the like.
I tried to make them into something on the paper,
A pattern, bring some order to a white sheet,
But no matter how I tried I could not re-create
The perfect pattern that caught my eye on the floor,
Only a few minutes after they came in the door.

Moving On

I refuse complacency in my life.
It is change, and change for the sake of strife
and in the calm, that is a false respite

I play with many jigsaws, the pieces
jumbled – family old and recent,
friends who come and go within their leases.

Have I scrambled faces for a purpose,
playing the bored god who purports
to calmly crust my won cauldron? These ports

in my seas – where I stop and take a view
and laugh at the cataclysms that I grew –
shock me to have what I should not have.

I am all fucked up and guilty for a while.
It will pass. I am a white witch who
reflects guile in the mirror of a smile.

Paddington 13:15

I want to be old and grey
and sitting on a train going somewhere,
and in the inside and outside heat
doze a little,
and dream fondly of how things were
and how things might have been.

Chaperone

The penultimate time we met was in a bar
without an audience. We talked about
the girls and agreed some tactics. We even
laughed when we forgot who we were with.

The last time we met was in your house.
Your auditorium. Your stage where you can
shout: *Get Out!* The girls, your audience,
had gone outside to check out my hired car.
You smiled then alright – a lost opportunity.

That was a narrow escape –
you using words to rape
the gesture of an easy exchange.
I was lucky that time. Never again.
Next time I'll bring a chaperone,
wheel in a barbed wire fence,
and talk to you by megaphone.

Too Early to Explain

There is in this a depressing ache,
a bereavement. The Styx has been crossed
and a best friend is elsewhere. There is no bridge.

Words are no longer smooth between us.
They are now arrows seeking the softer places.

We no longer see each other without the tripwires
of you said, I said, you thought, I meant.

The children stand apart to personify our loss.

When will actions be a pleasure again and not
be wished away to satisfy public bereavement.

When will we reach into the subliminal comfort
of our enjoined history and know again.

I did not mean to break our special pact,
I just felt around inside and it cracked.

There must be a time to put away the weeds,
for hell is never. Like a seed, the shell
around the ache is a terrible loss.

Doing the Sums

I can still dream. I still have that.
Big dreams about millions, about name recognition,
Not so much about face recognition. Not the face.
You have dreams too, compacted into *one, two, three,*
This is where I'll be in five years time.
You can call it ambition as if it is more real.
Still sounds like a dream, only with bullets.

I think I am where I wanted to be at this time.
Could have softened a few edges here and there,
Been a bit pointed about a pension and regular
Income and things that may matter in the future.

Could have worked harder at us,
But always thought I did. Now I'm not so sure.
I remember the newness, and then the maturity,
And then the ease of passion and ease of being,
And I remember only the good times
As if memory plays tricks and rubs out the bad.
I am sure, could swear, that there were no bad times.
Now is that crazy or over-compensation, or luck?
Without you there would be no times. I know that.

Might be easier if I knew how many years are left
Then I could compute a percentage and say
This is about right for where I am now.
But if I die tomorrow, who will remember,
And if I am only halfway through, who cares.

In the Dark

It's at the end of a passage of time, a turning,
A date to remember perhaps,
A day to remember that squirrels threw
Yew berries at me, high and nameless
They all look the same to me.

And all around the dead leaves and wet bark,
And the dirty needles
And the bits of fence that need painting,
And the confluence in the corners
That is enough to put anyone off.

It will be dark soon. It can wait until then.
And then it will be too dark to see.

And you are in between jobs, resting.
I give you a week and you will have a list
Of those who love you and those who don't
And the recklessness of decision-making
Should take up most days until the only
Decision acknowledges itself.

All other options are off.

Somewhere a Star

Night is starting to replace the day. Summer
is done and it's time for a change although
I hate the cold and I hate the hibernation.
I suppose I hate the dead of it all.

This is going to be a dry week - last night
no drink for the first time in years. Not that
I have a problem, I just enjoy the stuff too much.

Early November, and the lists are starting.
Some radiators need draining, the front door
jam is letting in a draught, there is a small
leak from the flat roof, could be condensation.

I wonder will I get the shakes by the weekend.
I fear if I do it will say something I don't
want to hear. The only cure is another beer.

It is a time for action, the busy selling season
is on us. Up early today like most days and
at my desk, got some requests out before
eight, phone calls to Europe before nine,
clear desk, clear head, full 'to do' list.

But it's early in the morning. I started too soon.
I never drink at noon but it does get dark early.

Early November, you can hear further now that
the leaves are shed but not far enough for me.
Clear cold foreign sky. It never seems quite fair
That somewhere out there, a star will flicker dead tonight.

Running

I came back from the run and saw our house
and bent over to catch my breath – from the run of course –
but then I straightened up and thought you might not be there.
Just like that. Just from stopping to catch my breath.

The shadows are gone. The gutters are full of leaves, bunched
leaf tails snug to the edge and big sycamore leaves impaled on
broken nails in the fence and birch leaves along the driveway
like feed for chickens, and the green sward on the railings
disappears them into the laurel, and the gates –
just then I remembered hearing the hinges squeal even
though I was some way away. Even though they were closed.

I like the smell of the oilcan and the scrape of the brush
along the path, the wet cleanliness of the leafless, the gush
of the water as it releases into the down-pipe, the smell
of the dead when the brackish is cleared of leaf lumps.

But if you were not there, who would admire the work
or lift a leaf that missed the brush? Where would the colours go
and the sound of voices, and your touch on my arm:
where would they go if you could not be here?

Then the lights came on. Sudden like, and you moved
in the kitchen, moved from chopping board to stove,
and the light caught the light in your hair
and I could see your lips move as you sang
and I wondered how it would be if I wasn't there.

Digging a Drill

First week of December we'll
plant the English hedge.
First week of December when
the roots are dormant.

I dig the trench I should have dug
a few weeks ago. Now the frost
has hardened the ground and I need
a pickaxe to get below the crust. I can
smell the horse manure that's piled
up over there. That's next.
I dig faster to blunt the smell.

It was like being in that hotel.
Water dripped all night like it knew
I was easy. I opened the window to let
in the motorway and obscure the sound.

It was like that year. I should have moved
out in December in the transplant time.
Maybe they wouldn't have noticed and
I would have been in the clear.

Digging a trench digs up more of a hole
Than horse-shit can fill.
Maybe leave it another year.

The Itch

It has been noticed, you know.
Oh Yes! It has been noticed.
How long since you took care,
Or asked did I put cream on my face,
Or cared about my cuticles,
Or folded my shirts before a trip,
Or met me naked at the airport
With only your coat to hide your game.

Who makes the meal more often now,
And who only notices at the end,
Who tots up the price of presents
And says it doesn't balance,
Who kisses the air and misses my lips,
Doesn't say *headache* any more,
Just rattles the box of pills?

How long before you care again,
And dare again to make it in the dark,
To surprise even yourself
With your brazenness.
The red baron comes more often now,
Summer seems to be a long winter,
The evening meal is a video treat
And we only meet when we have to meet.

Does everyone else go through this?
We slipped into it unawares
Even though we said we'd care.
I don't think it's too late to change our ways,
But it has been noticed, you know.
Oh Yes! It has been noticed.

Argument

You are away now, working harder for us,
and maybe for yourself if you are honest,
and you permit me the free time,
an indulgence in abstinence to make my own.
Hard words.
I can phone about the changing leaves,
the red berries from the yew,
the first slivers of ice on the pond,
our daughter's ten millionth step
which you missed at this turning of the year.

I thought of collecting stamps again
so I can keep up with your travels,
but what use are stamps on cold nights
when the window is open as I like it,
when the sheets are damp as I remember when a child,
at the haw that I get when I breathe passing our large mirror,
and return to try again when the shade does not notice.

All this I could do for you,
all this I could snap with a digital camera,
but where's the use in that.
No camera for snores, or bugs at the front door
where we watched a spider catch a fly.
No camera for a sigh, no focus for unplanned.
No need for any of that.

I wonder how you reconcile the passing with the past,
with a stop by John's grave for example
and work the maths of years lost and what will happen when,
if it could. The future continuous without a wake.

I swept the leaves again tonight –
in case you came home early and slipped –
what an old man thing to do. The young never slip,
or never seem to seem as if they do.
And when I came in I tried to fix a bit of your jigsaw
but the preponderance of black confused me –
how can you see in from the edge?

But the stamps,
well these alone are mine and the pretty pictures
and the celebration of historical events:
I am all for that.

Dreams

So what's wrong with changing a dream?
You say it is like keeping your eyes closed
beneath a balaclava, encouraging a stream
of consciousness that owes much to my roots,
but not so much that even Joyce could bear.
There is no obvious conclusion
When you are stalled in relative latitude,
in the middle distance, your own illusion.
I suppose there is no value in saying it is a different view,
no colour, easy to replay the life and times
as I want it with my pliable cast of a few.

I find myself dreaming more by day now-a-days.
The year is cutting in and the air inside the house is sleepy.
My mind wanders aimlessly through this and that
and I suppose if I put it in a poem it is not so bad,
but sometimes, I just let go and come up with crazy things –
like we will all get on,
you and your ex, and me and mine,
and your ex's ex and all the kids,
and I even see the fun of cross-marriages
where we have to explain this is my ex's ex's
first child once removed, who's now my grandson.

And I can replay the conversations to where
nobody cares who leaves what to whom,
and everyone nods to the positive in everyone else,
even when they have left the room,
and every negative requires a re-take.
If only every day could be like an Irish wake
where you say things as a truism, like
God be good to him, but he wasn't the worst.

I suppose it is an insurance policy in case you leave me.
I would still like to be invited over for tea
and I promise to provide the agenda and opening paragraph
to get things going, and you can tell the silly stories
about me that you know will make them laugh,
and I will gild your charm and your beauty with words,
and say positive things to the gawking herd.

But they will only reply on their way home,
and wonder aloud then what you saw in my dreams,
and wonder that a man like that could dare
to dream, but nothing is ever as ever it seems.
And all this because you introduce me as your ex,
but with feeling, like a special ex.

When You Really Know It's Over

Áras Uí Dálaigh, Fourth Floor,
Reception Area.

The Civil Service chairs,
and chipped coffee tables,
chipped walls and stained carpet.
Yesterday's paper
folded on the floor.
Staff only on the door.

Around the corner, her
solicitor and mine,
a wig to mediate.
She's confined to her room
and I'm in open space.

Brief me quickly, he said.
And then I condense the
twenty-five years of two
very uncommon lives
into a numbered list:
this for me, that for you.

Wondered would it make sense
if I computed a
fraction of the great times,
divided by the hurts?
91.2%,
the balance, carried over.

Why can't we rescue talk
from bumbling retainers
and end our marriage as
we entered into it -
with a ceremony.

He's back, we talk, he's gone.
We haggle the full stops,
give and take the commas,
agree bricks and mortar,
pensions and policies
are easily seen off.
But the children,
the soft underbelly
that defines us, becomes
the final battleground:
the little person on
whom we should agree, we
thumpingly disagree.

Nothing is agreed, then.
We'll write to you.
                    Thanks.

Looking Back

I did not drink so much last night so why
did I awake into the nether grey
just after four – not quite another day.

The sound of quiet breathing and foreign
noise outside levitates this forbidden
time. I've never woken up at night and
been happy at awake. Behind my head
I settle in and cross my father's hands –
a sudden rush to steady myself, I
have enough without unearthing that dead!

I cannot hold the same thought for long as
if I am balancing on river logs.
Was I disturbed by groaning wood or dogs
barking? They release problems in their wake.
I know the positive step is to make
a list, draw lines to solutions and scratch
the problems out – take a management view.
There is perversity in watching who
is damaging whom in this verbal game:
the badly advised will argue for gain,
the other will be righteous and aloof.

Where are my daughters? The baby mothered
will be asleep for sure but the others –
who knows? If ever I had a right I
have none now to question who they are with
or when they got home. We do not have time
to exchange and learn. It is all behind
us like a fleet departed but I would still
like to interfere, to approve at will,
to criticise and be taken seriously,
to enjoy the argument and the thrust easily.

This must be what it was like when men went off
to war and children grew up without knowing.
We had advantage, the easy growing
time, lots of time, as much time as we had laughs.
Now we meet like close relations in cheap cafs

that have time stamps and we fill in the hours
to an agenda that never was ours.

Our common disadvantage is our bond,
my late wife, late lover, late friend. Her craft
is her bitterness using words as darts,
using friends as fools, using lawyers as bait
to sop up cast-offs and regurgitate
what he, the nameless he, did last to her.
I thought until recently that if I
was twenty I'd ask her to be my wife,
ascend in ignorance, descend to grief.
Now I'm not so sure.
Wandering in the morning makes me grieve,
but not this. It sours with the vicious touch
of a blowtorch on paint and makes me heave.

And in between these webs, these many takes
rehearsing life, we have money bitches,
demands fore and aft, and brinkman issues
and yet we need lawyers? Give me a break!
How right you were when you said: *If you had
died we could have wept, the insurance would
have wiped the slate clean, and I could have dressed
with the respect that only widows can.*

Enough. I have more immediate plans.
Important people like the Vatman
visit. I think they think I'm on a scam.
I spend some time on who says what and why
as if I'm their single focus today.
Credit letters take more crafting than
a poem would get because much that I care
so little for is in play. He'll sort it,
always has done. Pass the buck. Pass the blame.

I count the hours of sleep and know it will be
a long, long day and then the radio
comes on and I switch it off quickly.
Five more minutes or so,
like stretching exercises before a run,
and then I must up and face the dawn.

Passage through Time

If I could have done things differently
I surely would. This is the parallel litany
of everyone's reclusive life.
The half muttered excuse,
the great *if only*
and the conjugated last words
as if that is all that could be left,
as if leaving itself is not enough.

When Uncle Paddy died he lay in a room,
the room where he had slept most of his life.
The last cough smear of where he slid down
the wall must have brightened the dull wallpaper
until he was found and it had dulled back brown.

When I visited his house it was not
the dark smearing where he stood,
or the damp odour and disinfectant,
or even the latent smells of childhood,
or how small the house had become –
it was my grandmother's hat and coat
still on the hallstand as if she had gone out
that morning and forgotten to put it on.
She was dead some ten years by then,
and of my grandfather – nothing.
She had carefully cleaned him out.

We loved what she loathed,
the bread smell and cosiness
of his Guinness breath
and his big beer belly
and his warm clean hands
and his Evening Herald –
a simple breadman.

She was a tough woman,
and Paddy, well he just lived
in a world of his own,

cigarettes and chewing his nails,
more reclusive after he retired,
and we were just busy I suppose.

I thought about them recently
when I thought about us,
about how things should be,
about how things are not the way they should be.

I could have been more prescriptive,
followed a plan, set some steps along the way
and maybe everything would have been fine,
nobody hurt. I could have done things better,
well some things differently at least.

I missed the milestone where it is too late,
and the plan seemed to be just my plan. I waited
for a better time, for a right time, and thought
too deeply and too long. That which you sought
should have been well delivered. At least I think so now.

Do you think my grandparents had plans,
had dreams in the dark and thought great thoughts,
had ambitions for their children, grandchildren,
cared deeply enough? Something snapped. One day,
just one day everything came apart
and irretrievably that was that.

Who remembers them now,
where their separate graves are
and how high are the weeds?

And what happened to her hat and coat?

I would like to know these things,
like I would like to know
what wall I might slide down,
and maybe do some wailing at it now,
before I have forgotten how.

Carpe Diem

Ocean snoring, grass singing,
Somewhere a child is whinging
In her siesta trance,
And a dog whelps the ire
From another disturbance.
In amongst the Spanish quick-fire
I hear Cockney and Wiltshire.

When we had those words last night
Then re-joined the others,
Did you look past the guttural
And think, as I think today,
That that was the final run
Of the premier of this play,
Wasted on an audience of one.

Japanese Meal

It started with Sushi, raw fish on horseback,
And ended with a dessert never touched,
And I noticed you smile like you used to
And I wondered if we were on a new tack.

Six people for a dinner party.
The ideal number where none can hide.
We had not had one for quite a while,
So little practice for the complexity
Of many courses of a tricky meal.

We discovered a new martini –
Equal measures of sake and vodka
And a very thin cucumber slice –
And everyone agreed that the
Cucumber was a defining choice.

I am sure they are correct but I
Could only taste cucumber.
The nuance of a mixed oily glass
Leaves me cold since I got drunk
On schnapps and put my hand
On another girl's arse –
She took it away but you noticed.
I only know this because you told me.
But if I wasn't there sober
How can it have happened?
Here was history repeat itself from last year,
Although she was only half a couple now
And carried that recent bother.
We were still mixing shorts and beer
And convincing ourselves that one
Offset the dehydration of the other.

The sushi is uncovered – a dish
Of red and yellow and white
Over balls of ninety-nine grains,
A dissertation of raw fish.

To the table then and sit where told.
It has already been decided
Who will talk to whom,
Who will conjoin and dissemble,
Who will make good partners,
Even within the obvious stricture
Of man, woman, man, woman.
The hosts have made a judgement
And nobody dares change position.
The tablecloth is white with black
Place mats, a starkness that could affront.
But then it's Japanese, and that is perfect
When carefully planned to be casual.

A Japanese meal without miso soup
Is not a Japanese meal –

It is like marriage without sex,
Or love without touch,
Or conversation without words,
Impossible to imagine,
Impossible to conceive.
But when do you call it something else,
An oriental meal perhaps,
Or something from Japan?
Which sound like *we are just good friends,*
Nothing to worry about,
We regularly call,
No change to ingredients,
No change at all.

The least amount to eat is always
The most difficult to prepare.
The little shitake mushroom,
Hunched over sea-weed and tofu,
A tooth filler wrapped in leaves,
With a wasabi kick and distant taste.

Like something remembered,
But who and when and where?

The ricochet of plates
Took the image away. But now
I am thinking hard and I cannot quite place
The place or time but it was there.
Something stayed in the memory,
A pleasant reassurance from a taste,
Like remembering Africa from its smells,
Each step a carbolic friend,
Or the dust smell before or after rain,
Or the lushness of the new grass
And its sweetness when you step on it
Like it is exuding the first thrusts of grain,
And the Frangipani around my past,
Around the windows and the stoep,
And daughters crying their first cry
Like mantras to an African sky
And the confusing sweet smell of new baby
In a mining hospital before the rains stopped.
But these were not wasabi, bwana,
Just the memory of a memory that is done.

The carrot sherbet was a big success,
The sweet cold diffused our tastes,
The expectation of something great,
Even a second helping –
Of sherbet? For goodness sake!

And words had followed words
And time moved on as people grew
Easy in their imbibing hues.
A stab at politics. Even though we all
Read the same papers, we confirmed
Our grievances and prejudices,
But jousted a little at first to find the
Open argument, the soft places,
Before striking with a smile.
I wonder is that the way it is
When surgeons confirm a melanoma,
A challenge to find something new,
A dictate for the text books.

But I know these adults here,
And in one-to-one we each of us care
Not just a little but a great deal.
But here we have an agenda
For the table, and it's not how we feel
That counts but how we surrender
To someone else's better-held view.
Maybe we could learn at a Japanese
meal to do as they would do –
Incline graciously to the wiser head
And use another machination
To see him dead and still keep face.

A full table can be a lonely place.
People drift in and out of words
And in and out of different states,
And hide behind the contemplative smoke
Of an in-between course cigarette.
I wondered what my daughters were doing
Just then, could or could not be here;
And some word woke a dead friend;
And another my mother's obituary,
And I listened carefully to hear her knock;
And they spoke about kids and antics
But they are all at home for them
And my ten-year age gap has its gap
Where kids move on and we become
The front line – but how can I tell them that?

The main course is set –
A monkfish pattern with a butterfly design,
Intricate vegetable spreads and rice,
Nothing out of place, nothing untried.
Mouths fill and words are in decline,

The host tops up the wine
And everyone agrees it is the best
Japanese meal they have ever had,
And that's when I saw you smile.
The main course is complete –

Some will leave and most will stay.
They have made arrangements,
The babysitter to get away,
(that's what my father would have done,
first opportunity and he's gone.)
The martinis and cigarettes are at play,
For play is what it is now,
A setting out of places, louder music
In case conversation is rekindled,
A breath in the wrong direction,
A light, a dance, a touch, a request
Perhaps to fill a glass or explain a thought,
A reaching beyond the mould.
Shoulders are rounder and backs are sloped
As if hearing is faulty and they must be in close,
And everyone leans into everyone else
And the ritual has begun to unfold.

And when I suggested dessert
It was already too late – another time.

You sit like a matriarch,
Sharing cigarettes and filters,
Topping up another's glass,
Listening but not receiving
Even when the gift is very personal.
And then the unexpected struggle
From your friend through her son's death.
She has the conch now and she lingers
Through that day, so many times rehearsed,
So many years ago but never over,
And we feel her loss which cannot be
Articulated as she would wish, drunk or sober.
Always forever there, always forever gone.
And somehow the conversation passed on
But the gap was left, like the gaps
In our own prescriptive lives,
Like the regurgitation of sentences,
Like a rehearsal of justification,
Like an articulation that will be perfect,

Like an engineered feat around a rupture
That will explain coherently the effect
To another party sometime in the future.

The hours moved round to three
And I suggested that we
Should all go to bed,
Especially as you said
You would be up to run
At eight or nine or whatever time,
And unusual for us we left the clutter
And went to the stairs and climbed and climbed.

A great meal, you said, well done.
A kiss, a hug for a longer while,
And then we turned our separate ways,
And I lingered on that moment when you smiled.

There is no us

They say that tangled threads of tweed
have a life of their very own,
yet are willingly thrust and sown
into patterns by the spinning wheel.

But when unravelled over time,
they gird the tangle - like lovers
stripped of their camouflage –
one loves no more, no more aligned,

as if but one of them had loved,
had loved in verse that's now destroyed –
spin and spun through one's denial
to places where old dreams are shoved.

One comes to the cliff edge and flies –
the other had no need for wings
so stands to mourn and hoarsely sings
of love that tragically died.

You say: *move on now without fuss,*
in that all passing passes thus,
hug to forget, just don't say us –
all change, all change, there is no us.

And this, our troth-ship dead on lies,
like berberine beads of colour
on a widow-weeded cover,
as final as a taut goodbye.

The Sunset

I cannot get it out of my mind –
The drip cooped parallel lines across
The photo grain, carved forever in
That one photo of a Donegal suite.

It's a signature really, a scrawl
On the perfect sunset-mirrored lake,
The causal greens and themes of red
Observed in silence by two wan men.

The kids are asleep in the car. Kids?
A young man who could yet be called up,
A young woman of child-bearing years,
And the kid – thumb in, silky sucking.

The two men, absolved by time
Lean against the car and meter
The setting sun – arms akimbo,
Chin stroking from here to Canton.

But they miss the nearness of lines,
Miss the lives in the white houses
Beaconed in the shadows over there,
Miss a woman fondling her neighbour's son,

Miss an early rosary against the chair
Like in the olden days, safer days,
Miss an early tea, a farmer come in,
Miss the love of eyes, translucent thin.

I thought of you that evening on
The anniversary of our away
Through bested lives, parallel or not –
God, I missed so much last year.

I wish now I'd put my finger in the frame –
We could have laughed at that before –
I wish our dreams had not been lined,
I wish that wishes came in fours.

Christmas Haiku

We did what we did,
Regret's more scary than failure –
Holly, mistletoe.

Love and Other Distractions

Reflection

I have found the godhead and it is myself -–
I am the dancer, the dancing and the dance.

The evening my friend's wife gave me flowers
(for Rosalind)

Herself a friend.
This, the tall vase and the slip lip
Where the head of flowers
Bursts like an aching thrust –

And then he tried to tie
The eye of your string bracelet
And announced he couldn't find the hole.
That old excuse, you intoned.

And there it was. Said.
Like a sluice between the beers and tears
In a crowded bar. Inside the smoke-zone,
Seeing two public lovers
Touching with dept finger pressure
The moment that lifts them clear.

I love the freedom of that,
The power to reach far, far up
And release a bird from Alcatraz.
No permission to be or not permissive,
No hiding beneath the table-top now,
You in your regal after-math,
And he as graceful as an acrobat,
And neither quite coming down to earth.

What a precious moment to have empowered,
The evening my friend's wife gave me flowers.

The Fisherman

A Fisherman without fish to catch!
This lovely man, casting into the Dove River,
Stopped to chat when asked how it was going.
Yesterday was such a beautiful day that the May Fly
danced in their millions and the fish are full –
so full you could beat them with a stick.
They have no interest in my flies.

But I had.
He took his three packs from his jacket
And walked through a world of wonder –

This one here I tied with yellow silk,
And this is floss from a seal's itching,
and here is underhair from a hare,
and this – a quail's down after mating.

and I said, a number of times,
how pretty they would look as hair slides
or brooches perhaps
but he was having none of that.
Flies are not decorations,
They have work to do.

He had caught a few hundred trout
these past few weeks, just like that,
this man with his funny hat
and his pockets within pockets,
and his nimble fingers, rod nimble,
and his flies, all tied by him alone,
and the wonder of a world that travels
so far to emulate a fly so near.

This one here I tied with yellow silk,
And this is floss from a seal's itching,
and here is underhair from a hare,
and this – a quail's down after mating.

He said he was out more often now,
Since the wife had left,
Had more time to tie,
To think about things,
Life, that kind of thing,
And his eyes held mine just the once
But I hesitated and missed the chance.
Then he put a fly into his mouth,
Threaded the eye one-handed,
Spun and dropped it by a jump,
Then said: *I might move on to another place,*
And walked inclining deep up to his waist.

The Handbag

My Australian friend,
Ebullient as her country,
Feet plumbed solid for discourse
And sure, sure as sure can be.
We talked about handbags,
The paths of in and out through secrets,
Lots of untrammelled secrets,
And charms, yes, lots of charms,
Flotsam of magic interlacing hints
Of dated cutaways, a folded photo,
A calling card, a must-wrapped mint,
A train ticket to someone of late,
And an air ticket with a full-stop date.

An eastern woman overhearing
Said people would not be so flippant
Where she comes from,
Would care about politics and torture,
About life and death,
About bigger issues than handbags.
So we unrobed the metaphor of folds,
The zipped comings and goings
That riddle inherited traits and learned behaviour:
The whisper that you can be bold, but saved for later
Like each encounter is a prisoner of sorts.
This woman *is* her uniform, her country,
A stop and search intruder whose hands
Cannot unpick the pith of bounded dreams –
Her bland rebuke to underlings confounds
The secret place that places have for things.

And my friend's eyes showed big,
Big as her scrubland where small things hide,
Big as her night-sky where eagles glide,
Big as the property of an open bag
With years of surprise squirreled inside -
Like this photo of her on a Literary day,
Crumpled a bit now, some years since Hay.
The hand that took it and the eastern hag
Have both been moved to her new handbag.

Learning from History

In a Peak town, in his studio, you asked the artist
If those were pansies in his landscape,
And this sad man on a late Saturday said
Yes, then sold you postcards
And said the wrapping was pricier than the cards.
Devil's spit was a withered spray
That drenched us,
Derailed us from our day –
And if we imploded to our defence,
It was that harsh.

But let's play that again -
This man's words had uttered what he felt.
His low-income day in a dull studio had dealt
A blow, but you were hit.
In the car you slept the furtiveness of your hurt,
Some sighs from your foetal moon,
The defensive pain then carried to the lawn
And stung the nearest hand reaching past.
A man has no known way to sigh
Even if enduring moments slide him by.
He cannot align expressive grief to obvious links,
Like nettles and dock leaves,
Like the dark green smell in shadows,
Like words and their ill effect,
Like what to keep and what to discard,
Like which words define the past.

But let's play that again –
Why, when we mentioned age,
Did you sniff
At the wrapping and ignore the gift?

The Power of Words
(for David)

I

I bought my daughters copies of your book,
A father's prerogative, but not theirs.
They read it nonetheless.

I gave my daughters a gift of magic,
Dipping-in magic, of hope and finding places
And each in their own way found traces
That moved their lives along.

The Head Girl's intonation to her peers,
The next to stimulate a seeking mind,
A third to drive away unfounded fears,
The eldest to take a disabled line.

And all of this from jumbled words
So many to a page, so many pages to a book,
In some order around chapters with no order,
Not quite a price per pound,
Not quite fridge magnets,
But then, not quite not.

II

Is this book a spell of elfish dust
Or the carking throw of dice,
Or musty bones perhaps, or upending tea-cups
To see what might have been, or may be,
Or is it honed on tales about fear
That have done you and us no harm?
Well, as long as we cram shut
Like tight silage in black bales,
We are the harm we do ourselves.
How easy when sins were worse
And the priest measured his terse
Forgiveness as so many prayers,
Until the next time of course.
We gave up a cheap confessional
For a far more expensive box.
So now? Where do we go now?

III

I escaped into madness in a heavier tome.
An earlier Ulysses defined a brutal route
That became James Joyce's dipping book
And that does it for me – a burrow perhaps
To a more threatening time, confused
By great contrivance in a Jewman's day.
I know those Dublin places, know them well,
Know the times of events and links and why,
And could explain each sentence if I tried.
But I find something every time, which is strange
Because I never knew the sense of loss.
Like going into a library looking for a book,
And then seeing so many, many books.

IV

There is something agnostic about reducing
Complex issues to a few simple steps.
Get this bus, that train, look for this street –
See where you want to go, and go there.
But how many pages in a train timetable,
Or a bus schedule, or the London guide?
And what use if you are dyslexic,
Or graphic bound, or apoplectic, or blind?
And how many ways to interpret as we're told
The special books of the religious fold
Who have dominated our lives with real fear?
And then someone says the message is simple –
Jesus loves you, or happy hereafter with Allah,
Or you are one of the chosen few.

V

It is just as well you wear black
And an open neck. No white collar, no studs,
No purple periphery to clothe your mystery.
We can single you out easily and measure
The charm of words that toss us about.
We can tuck our thumbs in the magic fruit,
And transpond the gift gifted by your book:
It is my vision, my starting block, my route.

My Favourite Things

Sunday morning in bed,
The newspapers scattered and a mug of tea,
Conversation over dinner, that magical gap
When someone says: *I disagree.*
A book with a happy ending, or not,
Or one where I just get lost.
The sunrise hours on my own,
The power of pen and poem,
These precious gifts that still surprise.

The phone call from my Mum. The latest news
That mrs-so-and-so has flu,
And my sisters, rehashing childhood feuds,
Unaware that we are broken records too.
A pint of Guinness slowly poured at home,
And going home, yes, and dinner with my girls,
My special friends, my equal and my mentors,
And then sitting back to see my DNA unfurl.

The curlew's cry on Sandymount strand
Just swells my heart. I no longer feel apart
When strangers say *good morning.*
Picking up a theme that unravels into verse,
And smiles, and children's laughter –
And bedroom giggles when the years reverse.

The wake that celebrates a good life's flight,
The flow of homage tears, the moment to reflect
On dreams, not those of the gnashing night,
But day dreams where everything is near,
And rational thought is mythically clear.

And these hands, these hands that count the gems
Who are my playmates, my listeners,
My crutch, there throughout and at my end,
These, these above all, my friends.

Youth
(for The Book Club, London)

I've been invited to a looking-back event,
To youth, looking back to youth,
And I am surprised that it should be looking back.
My first wife hopes I reach puberty before she dies.
A former partner told me to grow up –
But *grow up* in that confused way,
And could not when pressed, say how or why.

Shaw said youth was wasted on the young,
And manifestly aged it with a badge,
But each day I look in the mirror
And see teenage pimples in my father's image!

Perhaps youth is an attitude, a passing-through place,
A place to stop and catch our breath,
To look at the map and see where we go next,
And then go there - like a glider seeking an uplift,
Which cloudbank lifts best and which wing
Hints that the turn is right or left?

Down below I see people with both feet planted
Firmly on the ground,
Growing roots where they stand,
Dictated by their seasons, aged by being unsure,
Dicing time into what may or may not endure.
People growing people to be like themselves
And to partition their lives as they do their fears –
Youth, then middle age, pension, death.
And they say: *it's a safe bet* –
This is the way it's always been done,
Permission to leave, permission to return.

There should be a Government health warning
On the young wanting to be old,
To be settled, have kids, house, partner,
Following one dimension where the only tack
Is looking forward to looking back.

The Other Side

We walked into a cave, and then on into a tunnel,
And he did not stop or look back.
No words to explain, no words,
But crunched on the hardcore into the blackness.
I could not see and followed the sound of his boots,
As much a man as he, I would keep up.

Then the hole on the far side, a drunken exit,
A bit off but then maybe not, and of course not.
We walked out, and slid down the mucky mountain side,
And laughed like little boys, and washed some muck off,
But not all of it, a badge perhaps, a passing through.

The Wedding

Going to a wedding today.
Some excitement.
New tie, new dress, lots of newness.
And rushing, lots of rushing,
but in an ordered way –
To a timetable that we evolved into.

Got the car valeted. Nice couple.
Hope they're happy.
Hope it lasts to one grave.
But then what's new?
Already have two kids,
House, jobs, furniture – arseways really.

Not like in my day,
When you fell in love before sex,
And married before sex,
And everything was new,
Even the concern about the first time
On a day with lots of first time concerns,
And the long slide into a marriage
From which there was no escape,
At least not in my day.
The slant is different now,
More for them in their quiet anointment
Than for us – the witnesses.

Ready to go – new tie, new suit,
Same car, although valeted.
Some woman. Great in the new dress.
Should be a fun day.

Errigal
(for Jairo)

We came to the mountain.
Some excitement, lots of apprehension
Not so much tension as I lead
And the others follow, not necessarily in that order,
Like the lead in conversation,
He who has the conch, leads the thread.

There is a great deal of trudging,
Picking the hard footprints in the frost,
Then stepping on a print that is lost
In a wet slushy laughing quagmire,
And you know the wet when the cold slips in.

We stopped to catch our breath,
Or, being men, to let others catch theirs.
Then it's revealed,
The bare loneliness of a barren hill,
whitewashed in this early year,
And the sky, as blue as blue can be,
Interminably blue before the black above.
And the kids complain, and ask again:
How much further to the top?
And when I say it's the trek that counts,
They shoulder contempt as only kids can.

We stopped at the summit, had a snowball fight,
A far better way to energise the air.
A man passed by with two skiing sticks
Wouldn't stop to share our bread,
In too much of a hurry to conquer the spread
Of hills from here to Aghla More,
And we watched his traverse, marvelled at his speed
And wondered aloud at such flight.

And on this ridge, alone among my kin,
I took off my shirt to dry off my skin,
Macho I suppose.

Then had this urge that I had been here before
That someone was standing quite close
And I felt a warmth like a sodium flare
Slide up my calf, massage my back,
A hand through my hair, a clearance of sorts.
Just a few lovely seconds. No more.

If I tell what it was I diminish its core,
All I can say is what it was not,
And if I talk about that, it's not eternal.

I am turned to look at these hills again,
The fox prints around the stumbling rocks,
The casual cascade of granite stones
Tucked pastels over a million years.
Look down there to the Poisoned Glen,
The greens of dark and light and the cloud
Skimming shadows across the whispers;
And the pointers one step too far to Tory,
Those islands of the north bay, a succulent
Orchard reflecting each season of this day.

Look down with me now at the heather and kelp,
Each finding places of comfort to hold,
And the noisy stream that wasn't noisy before
Rushing excitedly to another balm,
Like it knows where it's going before it gets there,
Something exciting I cannot quite grasp,
But what are they thinking, these clusters
Of weeds and rocks and water and sky?

The kids leaned down to drink and I did too.
The frosted bracken stroked my stubble
As St. Tomas's hand slipped into the wound.
In the dance of water there's a sudden calm,
A mirror space for a momentary man,
Confronting the face of a theist in trance,
I have found the godhead and it is myself –
I am the dancer, the dancing and the dance.

The Road Less Travelled

I

It is the time before matins
The time when the wind dies down
And birds take a deep breath.
A man, grey-haired now,
Opens his Latin breviary
And slows to the pace of his territory.

His moments are well-rehearsed,
Sanctuary slow as if the time
From start to finish is well ordained;
The pages and pauses,
The turning of leaf and step,
The sigh and the deep breath,
Then a looking-up moment to reflect,
Drained of his vocation,
He is feckless and faithful and tense.

I watch him, his reverence.

II

Some days I replay what went before,
Dreams that we had and might have had,
A little tempering over time,
But still the same refrain
With an end no worthier than the end of any book.
But that book was well bound –
Each turning leaf marked
With licked thumb prints,
The dog-eared easy economy
That built on chants and ritual
As pure as any ceremony.

I suppose it was the same before,
And before that,
Although those steps were more sprightly,
And the rush to read and record,

Get it all down before it could fold
Pastelled the obscure into tinted events
So that a memory of a negative
Must now be prompted,
Like a photo that turns up from time to time.

III

Either path I could have tread.
The gravel path is well-trodden,
Same-step-same every day,
A captured cat pacing in its cage,
Each thought exactly in its place.
The path I chose, though, is less ornate,
A few have been this way before
But there is no way to see the way,
So round the bend
Is always too far to ever go back.

IV

Like coming up for breath again,
A catch in a rush of gusto
When we scaled the cliffs at Contil
And the sudden wind caught our breath,
My hand to lift those last few steps
As if rough clefts could portend the waning sun.
And the fun of a less cautious hand
When the children moved ahead
And gave us space at the marketplace.
How did we get here,
We who have been friends for years?
We who read maps and make lists and organise?
Some tide shifted, catatonic at first,
And then the slow procession,
A Fiesta de Santa Maria,
Where leaving was too public
And staying for the end
A commitment too far.
And, yet, locked into ritual
The surprise was that we did stay
And prayed to our gods in our own way.

V

We have paths in our garden now,
Paths of our own making,
And plots and trips that still surprise -
Surprises that will enhance,
Four hands crissed and crossed
Change the pull into a dance.

VI

The padre's deep breath –
Goodness, how much is in that!
Why does it matter if he never knew?
I could tell him how different it has all been,
But he didn't listen then,
Why should he listen now?

Dead and Dying

He's in a sleep warp.
For us, still the damp white knuckles and
Snow curls. Quiet now.

Graveyards

When I die
don't bury me in a graveyard
with strange people.
I have had enough of withered disapproval.

Throw my ashes
in the Avonmore river,
above the ford at Glenmalure,
so I can drift forever
through weeds and reeds
and crawly things.

When I Grow Up
(for Tom, died of Leukaemia, aged 5)

When I grow up, I want to be a pilot.
Not an everyday, in-between checklist,
Going grey with the fright type
Of dependable guy.

I want to be Action Man let loose,
Peter Pan with dynamite,
And last Saturday, guess what?
I got my wings.

Five-year-old kids don't die.
That's silly.
We just learn to fly.
I can magic a spitfire now,
Dive below the phone lines on our street,
Clip Mach 8 on a Tornado turn,
Rattle to pieces the Boeing fleet.

Look up. Look up. Don't look down.

There I am a shooting star
Blotting out the mid-day sun.
I can piddle at the speed of sound,
Pull my rudder and fart out loud,
I am the laughing boy in the cloud.

Going west now, going west.

Over Mother England, Father Wales,
Over Powys, Gwynedd, Ynys Mon.
Down to tickle Merlin's beard,
Have some fun with Arthur's sword,
Challenge Lancelot to a duel,
Play hide and seek until I'm bored.

I am the King of Chiseldon
Ready to take my Camelot place.
And in the forefront of my forces
All my generals will be nurses.

Ollie will be in charge of Toys –
Lots and lots for two little boys,
And Mum will be Princess of Wales
(The position is vacant, you know,
so I cleared it with Lady Di)
And Dad, well he'll just be that, my Dad.

Going round now, going round.

Hush. I'm on a different plane.
No flaps,
No pressure cabin,
No oxygen mask,
No support system,
No fear, no pain, no dread.

I am the wise one now,
Knowing how little I knew,
Or you knew,
Or ever lifetime will know.
There are no easy words for passing through.
I am beyond your brief.

Since I left home last week
I hovered about
To help you all out,
And to make sure my folks
Didn't mess up my funeral.
But now I'm through
And it's time to say adieu.
I'm putting on my cowboy gear,
Lone Ranger mask,
White Stetson hat,
Silver 45s and golden spurs.
I saddle up my horse,
My white ethereal mare,
And as you leave this Church
I will ride elsewhere.

Look up. Look up. Don't look down.
Let go. Let go . . . I'm gone.
Far out in the west, Tonto is waiting.

A Poem of Continuance
(for the Sands)

I - Lists

If you sit on a hill on a fair day
You can see the cornfields shiver below
As a hand of wind zigs this way and that,
In and across the field and out again.

Our parent's kin have been down there before,
Clumsy over the dry-stoned wall, they scuffled
And trampled the corn, and plod-hopped the lumps
Where the harrow had missed the ploughed up sods.
Head up, just waving hands to guide the eye.

They seem to build a rhythm to their trek,
Then they slither and grope in the wet muck,
Spit angry that this is not a caked path.
What invisible wall makes them move left
Or right, mirroring the wind from up here.
There they grab ears of corn to stay their fall
But where is the support in breaking stalks?

Out come the fold-weary maps, but this is
Cursory, book-learning, be seen to do.
The easy comfort is to look back for guidance,
To wait for the chuck from parent's traces,
Or emulate those on less tiresome paths,
Or to bond lovers and let go the stems,
And dance awhile through concentric oases.

It is never as it seems, harder now.
As obstacles become like Napier's bones,
The walls on both sides seem weary away,
And the first flush wanes – more sure, less strident,
More prepared to stop and homage the sun.

Turbulence to calm but the beat repeats –
One wind slows, and then comes another gust
Leaping over the dry stone. But look now,
It seems familiar – this one could be us.

II - Christmas 1999

He's in a sleep warp.
For us, still the damp white knuckles and
Snow curls. Quiet now.

III - Breaking Loose

The man is in the boy, breaking loose.
You can see it in the
rugby shoulders and strong arms,
bursting through a cosset of down.

Yesterday's clothes no longer fit
for sure. The run has eased to a half-run,
decision-slow like a gallop into soft mud.

Too soon he will smash the shell,
too soon the moon is full,
too soon the longest day,
too soon the choices as the
wind surprises around the cloche.
And he, nose up to gauge the change
or, to consider more precisely
his rate of change,
will know that he is good for him.
You can see it already. Look now.

Poem for John
(and Siobhan and Colm and Shane)

I can't believe that John is gone.
I needed to see him yesterday
Lying on his ruffled sheet of surrender
Just to be sure. He is dead alright.

I spoke to him on many days last week.
He enthralled some journalists with his vision.
He was anxious before the fray, and like a child afterwards.
He was just excited about the business of business.

He had an order from Mexico –
Mexico if you don't mind! –
And then another and another.
He reckoned he had cornered the market
For Tea Tree in America.

He said: *The product is walking off the shelves in Ireland!*
And we have contacts to do the same in England.
He had plans, big plans, huge day-dreaming bursting plans.
Last week was a great last week.

And then he fucked it up by dropping dead.

MacCormack, I wish – I hope you are here
Just so I can tell you how angry I am.
This was not in anyone's plan.

So now we enter a time warp. After today,
No more things to add to being us. Sure, we'll
Regurgitate the old stories to laugh and cry about,
And they and you will get better with the telling.

I have the agenda already to hand.
Like the time you got your ears done,
The first cosmetic surgery in Ireland.

Nobody could see any difference
Because you wore shoulder-length hair.
We only saw your foresight when you were bald.

Or the business with Father Magee,
And the camping trip and the spaghetti,
And all the complex Bluebell imagery
We took down through the years like an open sore.
We probably saved each other a fortune in counselling.
It is a fine and full agenda and we will start today.

It's a funny thing about blokes. We don't say things
That in a primordial way we simply know.
Like saying *I love you* to another bloke.
Just not done.
I suppose now that you are dead
We can break the taboo
Because, like all your friends,
I did love you.

You were a practical man, great listener,
Easily amused, solidly daft, allowing loads of rope
To keep our feet off the ground.
A dichotomy man, a Southern Comfort man,
You left half-bottles in all our houses,
Like a dog staking out your patch.
Please come back and visit these far better tombstones.

So what can I say for me and all your friends
Into this gasping, awful emptiness?
Goodbye, I suppose.
Yes, that's it,
Goodbye, dear friend, goodbye.

Grandfather

He was a breadman, the last in Dublin to ride
a horse-drawn breadvan, his picture full of pride
in the evening papers, lost in the irony of being last.
Better than his first public photograph
when he was shot being robbed and hovered on the edge.
When the man wrote to him from prison,
he met him and forgave: A*nd if I was he, he would too.*
Simple, but terribly sure.

Here was the perfect Santa when he smelt of bread,
homely and round and excited by what he read:
What do you think of this?
pretending to be deaf when Gran said:
You'll fill that poor child's head with nonsense.

He drank too much, she said too often
when he came home from his daily bender.
Forty winks and I'll be as right as rain.
The liver overdosed and got him in the end.
If not, sure the drink would've, was his final refrain.

He was an ordinary man who whiplashed surprise,
like when his teeth rattled at hurling games,
or testing the day's first pint: *Now that's very nice*,
or teaching me to finger Mutt and Jeff frames,
or funding my bus fares with a half-crown each week,
or slipping a parcel of meat and *Don't let your Dad see.*

or touching ugly bruises with the purple stuff,
knowing they were not from playing games. Impotent,
my refuge was his anger when words were not enough,

He slipped away as he would have liked.
No trouble.
The church was packed and a new priest tumbled
through his indifference.
Outside, strangers shook hands with strangers
and the priest prised them on,
a grander funeral to attend.
We were confused by the banter
With people we did not know but really loved him.
For years my Gran, even in her dotage, would say:
He guaranteed a bicycle loan for a man.
And he never told me.

I remember the day he was asked by that man,
I was helping that summer and he conspired with my arm.
A friend of a friend, now don't worry your Gran.
It's only a signature, sure where is the harm.

Even in Old Age

Why do you hang over that bloody crutch.
You hold it with authority:
a pointer, mitre, baton, some
foreign thing of a forgotten crown.

You seem to have come of age in old age
as if you had always wanted to be there.
You are easier now with us, your distants,
and maybe even us reluctantly with you,
easier with yourself, the self-effacement done.

Could this indeed be your final crutch?
You have made such an unfortunate life,
but you have a poor substitute waiting:
a few more years to seek us out.

St. James's Hospital

You are quiet at last.
Lying in your month old coma; mouth open,
I can see phlegm where your voice should be.

But it is too late to speak now.
No hard words to blunt us. You simply
stole our childhood and it's done.

Yet, we have never been so close.
I steal touches in your long night
when no one else is there except me.

And when your daughters come we
embarrass our speak with silence on silence
around your stare, anxious that you might hear.

You are quiet at last.
These years of dread are done now
and with your curtain close we close our grief.

The Pearly Gates

My mother aged her frame these past two months.
I watched as she shuffled the short hallway,
Side-ways on, as if gale blown, furrowed grunts
To pull a plough-share leg that's gone astray.

As I bent lower to kiss her forehead,
Her shattered red eyes, like landing lights,
Guided me in, and I held her brittle bones,
Careful not to break on *How are you, son?*

She streamed the events since last I was at home
The pace of visits and the gaps between,
Of who brought news of this event or that,
And who said what, and what it really means.

I took a turn a week or so ago.
Your sister was great but it slowed me down.
No, I didn't! Sure what do doctors know?
I'll be right as rain. You have your father's frown.

I made some sandwiches, Sunday's meat,
The whiskey's where it always is, and poor
Mrs. Aldridge was found dead in her sleep.
Each morning now I count one neighbour less.

I took a fig-roll, a child's wrinkled hand,
While droned the list of dying and the dead,
And pretended with nods to have known them
And in a school-yard I might once have had.

I remember her young and foot-sure fast,
Quick-fire chat as we ran along behind
To catch a bus, or be on time for mass,
And men's heads flirting smiles to hers inclined.

A stroke chucked the bit of this proud Red Rum
And her left leg coupled a ball and chain.
Her mouth contorted as if chewing gum
And her clawed hand turned into alms of pain.

She laughs a lot less now, is sometimes grim,
Then seems to look through me, and I wonder,
Not for the first time, is she seeing him,
That leaning tower that tore them both apart

Then left her on her own, no longer whole.
I suppose he'll wait by the Pearly Gates,
And then the head-down prayer: *God bless his soul.*
I whispered for us both: *Let him bloody wait!*

Travels

But I can see him still,
That forward face, the slip-streamed hair,
Two hands wrapped braces, a charioteer.

Frankie

It should have been a fun to-do.
Did he shag her or did he not.

The elderly lady spoiled the fun
Snorting that Frankie was too old.

Even in a country where
Eight o'clock is nine o'clock,

This was too much. A bet was placed.
Fifty dollars on twenty-five.

The lady paid – a bet's a bet.
And Frankie came between us.

Opa

She is out there now gently snapping the
limp daffodil heads and tying the green
stalks in a knot. The folding enmeshes
like a cocoon around the foetal root
encouraging growth for next Spring. It is
only May, so sure Spring will follow Spring.

Like watching her watching the Opa at
a German wedding, she special like the bride,
he ninety years old and sparkle-tooth agile,
tipped on his shiny shoes as he waltzed the
women around, beaming in his centrefold.
How did he survive so long in Germany
of all places?

His shoes shine though the soles are not new?
See how he banks his body like a glider
reaching for the airstream, watched in concern
by the family - will he survive the night?

Watching her watching him: deep bow to the
old lady, smiles, sits down and takes his beer,
calmly rehearsed for three quarters of
a century for this special moment,
not a tremble in the froth until it
touches his lips, watched by the ageing family,
counting how many he's had tonight no doubt.
Isn't he great? Meaningless words where the
meaning is visible. *Someone should squeeze
those two blackheads on his nose*, she whispered.

What to make of this man, who does not talk
of the past - I asked and got some rubbish
about looking forward. The same response,
when a child, I asked about that picture
of Hitler above the Dublin fireplace,
the man a patriot who didn't fight,
hiding behind the prejudice of a

twenty year truce, morals merely on hold,
applauding De Valera when he signed
the book of condolences, nothing said
when the atrocities unfolded and
the picture came down in '48 to
make way for a new type of wallpaper –
distracted like the shine on the dancing shoes.

We drank the fine Franken wine and some said
it was too young, even on a bridal night,
it should be put down for five or six years,
and then it would be perfect to toast the
new century from the dusty cellar,
as ready as the daffodils: firm heads,
upright leaves, opening their chrysalis.

The man with the picture will be years dead.
Will the Opa and his shining shoes be dead?
Who will be there then to remember the dance
and the blackheads that no one would squeeze,
and the fine wine forgotten in turn,
and the snapshots of a century past with
too many names and the details blurred.

Pedro

The crossword face on a man my age,
An anomalous channel from eyes to laughter
Dipping below the skyline where his battered
Hat shadows his face.

Picture the deft hands folding the tobacco leaves,
A string in his mouth, tep-tethering the shank,
Smooth-rolling along the leg of his trousers,
And sitting, sitting in a tobacco-rolling stance,
And the delicate intertwining fingers of a man
Who had ploughed a field with an ox when I first
Came on him, and helped clean the blade,
And clean the ox in the stream, and tie her up
With jagged rope to an iron in the ground.

Picture this man who offers fruit juice with rum
To another man who has walked over a hill,
Shows, when asked, how a cigar is folded,
then breaks it when I ask to smoke it –
too young, come –
and takes out pencil thin cigars he folded last year,
and we have a smoke.
Few words to caulk the sense of it.
Picture these two men communicating with poor Spanish
On one side and no English on the other,
Just talking and pointing and laughing like old mates,
Like young children do with foreign children –
When do we gain reserve, when did I lose it?
I lost it on a hill in Cuba when I came over a rise
And met Pedro, a man of my own age.

Why?

Old people with their memories,
Beating the carcass of an old song,
But no easy translation from
Anzio or Monte Cristo to this.

And the man who tried to explain
His predicament with dyslexia,
Beat his chest to get the right word,
Beat his chest to be part of the group,
Beat his chest
But could see no more motive than us.

Why did they land in the Bay of Pigs,
So far from Havana?
We learned why, but not then.

And the man from Monte Cristo
Told of the Germans he'd killed,
And of his mates who had died,
And the lucky and unlucky fate
Of some rune locked into time.
He could still remember the fuss.
And the man with dyslexia
Beat his chest
But could sound no more motive than us.

The Cuban Irish Wake

Transubstantiation is a tenet of faith
Even if only discovered of late.

Here, the man in the black soutane
struts about in army fatigues.

A person leaving, whatever the reason,
Betrays the Revolution.

I followed my father's path to England,
Easier to let a man go in his day.
Sure, they all had the faith and
Clustered in tribes to spurn the stares –
Now we are emigrant importers again,
Lording the roads our fathers built.

While here the grandeur is peeling,
Old cars, old slogans, old fingers pointing,
Dated compliance as if no one's aware,
No friends to whisper in aging ears:
The wall is down now, we *can* see in,
And after forty years, the wallpaper
And the headiness are wafer-thin.

The Demo
(for Anne and Jill)

You can put a tablecloth on a cut bole
but it is still the solid block it was –
And listening to speeches on TV,
the posters out to agitate,
to demonstrate approval
before the first shift, we came back to this:
Agree or disagree it is still correct.

Wake me at 6, you said, and we'll join them,
an experience, a blast from the past,
a demonstration in Cuba of all places.

It rained – never bothered us before.
It was cold and dark – an inconvenience.
Too much to drink – a tiredness perhaps,
but put them all together and ideals lapse.

I saw what you look like at 6 am
before the door closed, the demo on hold,
everything on hold really, or at least under appeal.
We can debate as much as we like
but at some remove the politic is real.

The Gentle Man and the Sea
(for Tom)

The boat on sand was clumsy,
Clacking ropes slapping the beam
And the sail, like Guinness droop,
An inert blob bent to.

We pushed it on to the sea.
As it mounted the platform
It became eager, like a dog
Hearing its lead is eager,
So he tucked and chucked the ropes,
Uncurled the web into lapped lines,
Few words to me, just odd nods
To brace the surge of too-eager.

Oh, the view was fine; voices
Drifting from the beach amused
Us through the hours, conniving
Strangers in another room.

But I can see him still,
That forward face, the slip-streamed hair,
Two hands wrapped braces, a charioteer.
A handkerchief betrays the cypher
And his slip fingers arouse the flow
Where the thrust is spent;
He turns us round when the hue of blue
Or the ripples gallop out,
This gentle man, well into his years,
Coax caressing his magnificent mount.

When we came to land, we packed
And grouped for the airport, passed
Back to our familiar crowd,
Told the hours until departure -
And several times I almost reached out
To tell him of my rapture.

The Birthday Girl

While all the others sat around the pool
I escaped with Panchero to the hills.
Passing his house he invited me to
Have coffee with his wife, meet his daughter.

Show the album of your 15th birthday.
A gorgeous young woman burst from the girl,
Caught in a dozen alluring dresses,
Seducing the camera, seducing
Me as her parents admired each turning –
Sucking her thumb now in young girl's clothing.

Only so many adjectives for a
Beautiful girl, and not in her language.
Only so many ways to feel the ache of a long time.
Exhausted,
Until the surprise of the blank pages at the end,
Some photos missed, or lent to another,
Or maybe an exposure caught the light.

And later on our way back from the hike,
Panchero stopped off to shower off the mud,
To dress for his day job as chambermaid,
And I met with the others by the pool.

115

The Guide
(for Ivan)

How big is a heart?
We saw it at Bodyworld, easily weighed.
No greatness there beyond the physical.

There has to be something in us,
a soul perhaps of other persuasions,
an ephemeral measure that
is parent-learned,
is nation-built,
is peer-pressured,
is moulded around the person
who is willing, or maybe not,
to imbue this gyrating behaviour
into his own construct.

How big are you?
You are a colossus of your generation,
a monument pointing out monuments,
to see and hear as much as the seen,
ambassador of every trait that is you.

In Cuba, or London, or elsewhere,
the epiphany is the trajection.
This is an embodiment well won;
Cuba should be proud of her son.

Blokes in Pony Tails

Boys will be girls.
Just that.

Real men eat quiche,
but probably can't spell it,
do the dishes and make beds,
hoover when they can't avoid it,
cook for an audience.

Real men have egos
the size of their potential,
don't drive big cars that say
something about their intention,
strut on their catwalk when they must
have firm views on the Big Issues
and ordain the world
the way they used to in olden days.

Real men make profound statements like:
'When a stallion is fenced in
it's good for nothing but breeding.'

But blokes in pony tails,
unbalanced by a single earring,
dazed by the fame
of their own reflection,
have only themselves to blame.

Lost in a Crowd

The loneliest place is an airport.
There are too many clocks,
each one vying to make the kettle boil.
Below each clock a place to buy:
pharmacy, books, ties,
junk souvenirs for kids,
expensive presents for the guilty.
Behind each counter a faceless face,
not unfriendly, just not in.
This customer won't be back -
regular travellers don't buy tin.

The sounds of announcements
are queuing like planes,
Did you catch that name?
Was that our plane?
Don't leave the bags unattended.
I knew that's what it was.

The click-clack of trolleys.
How come the infirm always
get the ones with broken wheels.
People learn to drive.
Five bags per person but
only two will be checked in.
The rest is hand-luggage in case
of a crash and they need to change.

Writing address tags to hold up the queue:
Is it where we were, dear,
or where we are going to?
And this. *Whose name*
shall I use, mine or yours?

Conversations stubbed as
people pass you by,
much as they try
to let everyone overhear,
their words are arrows past a keyhole.

Parents who were too old
before their kids were born
push Calpol children round,
and grannies smile their senile smiles
and hope the kids stay on the ground.

And in this ordered disorder,
there are people on their own,
a married couple here and there,
stalled too long for fresh speak.
People with purpose, some who stare,
some who mind other people's business,
some in suits who glare
then stride purposefully to another place,
take out a portable phone,
check for messages,
dial engaged numbers,
say *damn* out loud for the captives,
make a note in leather bound,
close their briefcase with a resounding clack,
cross their knees and
turn the pages of pink newspapers
with a decisive smack.

People in droves from arriving planes,
pushing doors too hard to exit.
The economy class go to carousels
and are surprised by their bags.

People islands, lost between here and there,
people who are pissed,
anxious though planes have been
around for a hundred years.
If you took a few out would they be missed?

The monitor says she will arrive
at 15:55.
Just checking, just checking.

The Tower

If you want to smell death come to the Tower.
It is an old dead,
as old as the smell of defecation is new,
As old as the dead slaves
That were dropped dead from the Tower.
That kind of death.

The Cubans here about are blacker than elsewhere,
A legacy of unmixed relations,
For who would come courting here?
They sell trinkets and fine cloth to the tourists,
Reluctantly,
Like they know the sale will be a bad sale,
Or no sale at all,
Handed-down behaviour as sure as their lifeless past.

I look up at the sky and yes it is blue,
Blue as it was earlier,
And there is the sun,
But there is a cold around the Tower.
Does no one else notice it?
Why do the people not leave?
The indenture is over, everyone must leave.
Get the fuck out!

And the Tower.
I climbed to the top with my daughter,
Kept her closer than any other time,
Even though we were alone,
Kept her out of harm's way,
Told her to mind her head on the beams
Where they swung the corpses,
Told her to watch her step
Around the slime of a local defecator,
Showed her the far horizon.

I can see good reasons
For recording the deeds of the past,
For keeping big reminders that things have changed,
But not this Tower, not this place.
It should be levelled,
Then dug up and levelled again,
A thousand times perhaps
Until the smell of death is pushed back
To the slavers' hell from whence it came.

Politically Correct

A woman came by with soap
And we confused the deal
Of buyer and seller, a giddy step.

And I heard the chant of an earlier appeal,
A fellow traveller teased
The shadows of her purse:
I owe you fifty cents for coffee,
And you paid for my drink last night . . .

This correctness hung each day
Like a long rope pendulum
A little way this and a little way that,
A shadow on a penny.

When did a round of drinks
Become a sum of correction?
Is accepting a drink the last defence
To a man unsheathing his erection?
In these it's the pleasure that counts.

We are not Samurai goring
Into the softer place of balance,
With our foreheads creased,
The deep dark weighting,
Witnessing forever just the once:
The haiku and the method,
The correctness of place and time.
No half measures there,
No second thoughts,
No giggling over price, like the soap seller.

She is creating a market for soap,
A few cents here or there buys her hope.
No effort to be fair - that's her buyer's hell.
She's too busy selling smells.

The Tip

We don't want to make him a millionaire,
and they gave a fraction of everyone there,

broke down the group dynamic
but shared in the accolade,
and everyone, in good grace,
dropped their eyes to let it play,

but in their hearts an angel passed.

The Train

Everything lies where everything is,
Unordered fantail of concrete spikes
Simulates the explosive device -
A bit dove-tailed by the passing years.

Hundreds surrendered, a crew man died,
And set in sequence Batista's flight.

Later at Laguna, then Giron
Charcoal militia broke an advance –
The Bay of Pigs had the world entranced,
Huge events, huge events from little souls.

We drove past monuments to the dead,
Noted the names and the age they died.
Took photos where photos are allowed,
Saw slogans, heard speeches on TV,
Mere tourists among the masses that
Keep the men and memories alive:
Che, Cienfuego, reluctant Fidel,
And the ghost of ghosts, the man Marti.

Our guide, acolyte of anecdote,
Trots out history with bullish pride,
The tougher the conflict the more he tried
To mantra rota that governs his role.

He read aloud a chiselled letter
From Che to Fidel. We stood aside,
Like acolytes in wonder.
On this special day, 14th June,
Prepared to agree, easy as to why.

It is important to value this.
In every *ism* thanks has its price.
The man who sees the grain, then the field
Puts value on history's set piece.

And the train, where the click-clack stopped and
The cracked points derailed it forever,
Appears to be a full stop.
But supposing
It had not been blown up, no dead crew?
There would have been a delay for sure,
Then the klaxon bellow:
Another train is due.

El Ermita

I see them laid out like shades upon shades,
Gut-gravelled hills tortured with history,
Like disgruntled giants laid down to sleep –
And nearer, the green saturated day.

Such disparate fields for lives beneath me,
Cuba, twenty-first century, and we,
Travelling sponges of our middle years,
Know so much but not the Cuban way.

An old vested gardener sold me cigars, and
A clean-lined guide praised the revolution –
Both wanted the wheel to turn one more shift,
But each knowing why, put a finger to their lips.

Children

And Dad, even though you're gone,
is she still my sister?

Playing Catch

We played Catch with a tennis ball
and she ran and jumped and organised us
for she is only eight.

And you, one hand in your jeans were
worried what people would say
and then worried that you could not catch
and then you enjoyed the game.

This is the way it is.
One hand tied to your 501s,
eyes aware of the audience around
even if they are not aware of you.

I was studious and picked leaves
for that was why we had come;
leaves with no blemish
for someone else's posterity.

Around the rose garden and back again
the tennis ball was thrown and caught
and lost and found in the rhythm of the game.

On the bonnet of the car
I pressed the leaves in panelled grips. Tight.
While she, just gone eight, read the instructions,
and made sure I followed every step.

The box of leaves is in the boot
Screwed tight and dated with today.
The ticket with my flight the same,
Another city, another day.

Easter Saturday

She plucked wild flowers, finger slow, as though
By crushing them the bounty heads might droop
And die. Not eight, her little mind still knows
The delicate balance of life's short sloop.
Some twenty flowers grace the banks below
Kilmuckridge town. We search and pluck and troop
An hour or so. Some flowers there we know
And back at camp we classify the group.

By Easter day the flowers fade. At least
We learned their names before the leaves could die.
But who were we who searched the banks that day?
Two names on shadowed steps that barely creased
The grass. The hour was sought: for should she try,
Maturing grey, that hour is years away.

When the Children Went Back Home

I empty in the loneliness of being alone
now that the children have gone back home.
They got the train from Bray
and I cycled back the way I came.
Walk, cycle, ship and plane –
imagine you could have done them all she said
if only you were on a plane today.
They see me in a crowd, moving
emotionless into my busy slot.

I am hovering in Dalkey, trying to kill some time
because the ship does not leave for hours.

There is no silence in alone.
I am surprised at that.
It is a state beyond a state
but firmly entrapped in now:
Gannets cry on Dalkey island,
a boat stutters into the harbour below,
cars saluting cars behind,
a woman chokes her cigarette,
people pass and laugh and say
the same things they say every day.

We rushed our goodbyes and missed our kiss.
Ten days done of summer dreams,
Christmas won't be long it seems,
The collage you made will gather dust
and not be seen until next Spring.

Crewe Station

The train has arrived at the platform.
We finish our tea and scones and move
with a little haste, with a contrivance
not to haste in case we hurt each other,
and go up the steps and over the footbridge
and down the steps and check the platform
and the train's destination again and you,
a young woman in the first flush,
kiss me goodbye and say you'll be fine
in that grown-up dismissive way
that's supposed to mean you'll be okay,
and I give you more money than you'll need.

Crewe station - off centre England -
destination Holyhead and a boat to Dublin.
Crewe station - with carriages crammed
and the calm guard knowing when it's time
and the smells of diesel, the noises of coming
and going, the blasts of other pasts.

People get on the train and make a fuss
and then get off again with their cases
and ask a guard and he says platform 3
but you have loads of time. They hurry
anyway. And in our quiet through the window
you say I should drive on home that you will be fine
and I say 'safe journey' because I always do
and you sit in your seat and open a book and
give a restrained wave because passengers
are watching and trying to put us in their
comfort box. And I walk out of sight.

Crewe station, fixed in time. Just a meeting
place for trains and changing your mind, a halt
where you can get the next train going back.

Crewe station, a blink when the fast trains go
through. Its importance is to carry
the journey, like a cathedral or a warehouse,
places for the coming and going.

Twelve minutes before the train moves on
and we lose that time forever.
All aboard who are coming aboard.
Stand clear those who are not.
The young guard does not flaunt the power
of whistle and flag or the authority
of his red braid and permits the train to leave.

The carriages move forward slowly with
the people and their baggage. You look up
and wave and smile a picture to take with me.
Daughter, you knew I would be there
and we both know that it's going to be okay.

The train moved on and left a draught
that shivered in the gap.

Watching Me Watching You

I am at a swimming pool in Florida,
the last day, watching the hours go by.
One hour, two hours my daughters sit and read
out in the sun: *we have to get our sun tans today*
as if the last two weeks had no effect.
I am in the shade blended in the grey
careful lest my nose should burn, twenty feet away.

Two weeks from now I will spend on airfares
and B & B in Dublin to have two hours with them:
pitched conversation, questions and answers, how's it going.
We will enfold layer on layer of difficulty, face on face,
and they will have more urgent appointments with a friend,
someone seen only yesterday. Will we talk about Florida
and the comfortable hours that we spent, saying nothing?

We struggle through a relationship on spare time and words.
Words are not enough. Silence is comfort too.
I should see that today.

Yet the hours go by and I need to talk.

A Letter from Italy

Your letter was like the first draft of a poem,
running with flushes, tripping around buttresses,
bouncing with subplot and mixed tenses;
glass-splashed like rushed varnish on a window frame.
You were in a hurry.

Eight pages to summarise a lifetime relationship,
the father and daughter fetter
that needed twenty years
as background to a letter.

It took me five minutes to read and cry
and days and days to ponder why.

It was such a letter,
a letter that opened out and let in light
like a peephole into Tutankhamun's tomb,
dreading words that were crafted with a spade
and not a scalpel.
The letter ended and was good
for in behind breathed a softer joy,
the touch and feel of an adult child,
taking on the master
and running faster.

It was such a letter,
and only such a letter could leap from you
and burst brazen like water up a swallow hole
and drench us both.

It was such a letter, your letter.

My Sister

Are you still my special Dad
now that you and Mum have split?
and where have you gone from here,
and what do you do all day,
and how can I pray if you are not there
to say Amen, like you believe in it –
even though we know you don't;
and will I stop loving you,
the way Mom stopped loving you?

Did I tell you a goldfish died
and we took it out with the net,
but we couldn't reach as far as you
without breaking the bank or getting wet,
so we had to wait for it to bob to the side,
and its eyes were bulging in its head,
like tears had built up from the inside,
so I cried for it and Mum said it's only
a goldfish – but, dead is dead.

And I'm having dreams again
only you are not there to say:
Close your eyes and float like a cloud,
above the house, above the crowd,
and follow the road to anywhere.
I tried and tried but it's too far
to get to the place where you are.

The house is more empty now,
and Mum forgot the bin again,
and she and I are having rows
and then we hug to make it sane.
Her friends drop by for a smoke
and ask about me as if I'm deaf,
and whisper about what's broke,
and they know I know it's wrong
to smoke, and to whisper.

And what about my sister?
Do you love her more since
you see her more? I miss her,
even though we always fight,
but that's what every sister does
at her age, and my age.

And Dad, even though you're gone,
is she still my sister?

Phoenix

I

What snide words or careless deeds made you skid?
You were more focused on the art of tricks
than we. You made things appear and then
disappear, but you were only a kid
unaware that the moment was fixed,
and we were stills of smugness – at least then.

You named your first poem *silence* and when
we pushed a start, you kept a rigid stare
as if you and only you knew the height
at which you had attained the muse, and then
you said: *chorus*, and we knew where we were.
We may have laughed but you had a new sleight.

A score of years. We walk separate aisles.
The cult of Tsar and Marie Antoinette
ghost the interweaves of a tragic play
which, like all dramas, has a finale
with trashing words and done deeds and a rage.
There is a pause until the audience claps,
but last week the audience was on stage.

Supposing, supposing we had not known,
or knowing we had never understood,
or deducing, had understood too late?

The magic here is that you encapsulate
a new order where we can celebrate
the prodigal bonfire of our mistakes.

Your presence was kindling – you, a new you
when from your fire of words a Phoenix flew.
We come wiser to a new altar where
each silence is a gap in *we love you.*

II

Icarus left his father's side
and took a fatal flight
from blue to black.
His only sight
was the sight of the sun.
His only route
was a magnet to heat.
He melted his wings
and crashed to earth.

III

You are back on cigarettes again.
We can check on that delay to wake again,
in about forty years! Who cares.

In Africa they say that
the racks in the silt will fill when the rains come.
We will cry this rainy season then, and
broker a new alliance.
Maybe we will call it extended family.
Maybe we will call it something else.
Maybe you should christen it this time,
since you own the semicolon
that was almost a full stop.

Fly again, sweet girl, fly heady with all of us.
It is only the Phoenix's feathers that are singed.

Grasses

I

She is meticulous,
Selects the runt, the broken, the limp, the almost-ran.
Long stems too long,
Short too short,
Blunted edges, this, the first culling of
False Fox, Grey and Tussock Sedge.

She harvests the heath
Between a crumbling wall and rusting wire,
In and out of shady hedge and unkempt lawn,
Then smiles to see the in-rolled awns,
Perhaps not seeing them but knowing they're right,
Right about the leaf-sheaths and the veins,
Right about the downy junctions,
The soft-hued grains too easily groomed from
Ratstail, Dune and Bearded Fescue.

Out of the yellowish fronds
The path closes
Then opens in the shy bract –
Two glumes hugging the lemmas
Seeing and ignoring.
                                    Then your Amazon snort,
For snort it was at roots that would not part.
I offered to help, then helped with brute strength,
And pulled and bruised the shoots and bent
The stems and offered a fist of broken limbs.
Your plied slim fingers lingered
So as not to discard too much too soon of
Dogstooth, Smooth and Hairy Finger.

II

And here she ponders at the window.
Watch now!
Those golden grasses are held aloft, fanning
Her slim fingers lost in green ligules.

The sun eclipses her haloed hair,
And in the vase the sacrifice complete,
In Gloria Excelcis,
She celebrates the newness of her priestess role,
Something sacred from new-plucked grass -
Like a great reaching,
Reaching past the lesser rotting grasses
Cast upon the ley, the hillock, and the hedgerow:
Broadleaved, Wood and Alpine Meadow.

Rain

There is the woman in you –
and it has been there for some time,
as sure as the rains precede the heat,
as sure as the coming and going of seasons,
this, the period of one life.

But now it rains and we celebrate –
we knew it would rain,
could feel the pull in our temples,
the stretching skin, the growing pains
of pressure charging up the scales.

And the rush – yes, the rush of blood
when the tickled drops increased in tempo,
pushed a wind to warn it was serious,
stretched palm trees like warm-up athletes,
and great globs of rain bashed the boards,
thundered on the roof, made us speak louder,
drenched everything in minutes,
sent rivulets to seek easy places,
gathered around the new softness of puddles
bled in the hardness of an earlier rain,
each a sop, a stepping stone to renewal.

And I caught your smile,
and then your laugh,
your abandon with the rain -
caught it on camera,
you who wilfully never smile for the camera,
caught at that deepened moment
when the heavens opened.

And . . .

Some day a Goddess will unlatch this gate.

Moving Into No. 38

My shirt on the line.
Your neighbours smile at the colour green –
It's not surrender.

Keep Trying

You can't confuse me with words,
But you can try.
It won't improve by undressing,
I'm desperate, but not blind.
And leaping naked on top
Won't change my mind.
Nor tears, nor kissing,
Nor somersaults across the room,
Or from wardrobes,
Nor oiling deep into my back,
Nor perfume smells,
Nor pulling lobes.
None of these will fly.
You haven't a clue.

You cannot make me love you more
Or adore you more
Or hunger more
Than I already do.

Welcome

On the frame between the panelled glass
I screwed the knocker to the door,
Failte - a solid piece of brass
Smuggled into rural England
So visitors would understand
That welcome has no translation,
Like *feck*, or *grand* or even *craic*,
All just simple Irish statements
That knocking now means coming back.

Cobbler's Cottage

It's only half an acre. Even so,
It has no limit now for us. We see
Beyond the fog where memories recede,
Where latticed horse-shoe paths could come and go,
So sure that going out is coming home.
We measured out the metre this first year,
And traipsed our future paths like binding weed
Around our fate. We are no more alone.

I sketched the formal paths with you in mind,
My painting box a smile upon your smile,
Then found the plans from 1958
And knew my hand had not been waltzing blind
Across the page. A whisper had been filed:
Some day a Goddess will unlatch this gate.

Love and Other Distractions